The World's Greatest Teacher

A True Story About My Dad

by

Mary Jo Weegar

Bloomington, IN Milton Keynes, UK

AuthorHouse™
1663 Liberty Drive, Suite 200
Bloomington, IN 47403
www.authorhouse.com
Phone: 1-800-839-8640

AuthorHouse™ UK Ltd.
500 Avebury Boulevard
Central Milton Keynes, MK9 2BE
www.authorhouse.co.uk
Phone: 08001974150

© 2007 Mary Jo Weegar. All rights reserved.

No part of this book may be reproduced, stored in a retrieval system, or transmitted by any means without the written permission of the author.

First published by AuthorHouse 1/31/2007

ISBN: 978-1-4259-8956-9 (sc)

Library of Congress Control Number: 2007900326

Printed in the United States of America
Bloomington, Indiana

This book is printed on acid-free paper.

The Lord's Prayer

Our Father, which art in heaven,
Hallowed be thy Name.
Thy kingdom come.
Thy will be done,
in earth as it is in heaven.
Give us this day our daily bread.
And forgive us our trespasses,
As we forgive them that
trespass against us.
And lead us not into temptation;
But deliver us from evil:
[For thine is the kingdom,
The power, and the glory,
For ever and ever.] Amen.

(Luke 11: 1-4)

This book is dedicated to the "love of my life", my husband, Tim, and to my two amazing sons, Andrew and Ben. I cannot imagine my life without these three precious people. I love you all to heaven and back. Thank you for your patience with me, encouragement, support, prayers, and most of all, your love through the writing of this story.

Table of Contents

Chapter 1:　The Beginning 3

Chapter 2:　The Garden 19

Chapter 3:　Environment 27

Chapter 4:　Encouragement 35

Chapter 5:　Memories 43

Chapter 6:　Educational Dreams 57

Chapter 7:　Time 71

　　　　　　Saying Goodbye 81

Chapter 1

"Set an example for the believers in speech, in life, in love, in faith and in purity." (1 Timothy 4:12)

The Beginning

As a young girl, I grew up in an environment of peace, love, and joy. This environment was established and made possible by my dad. I did not realize the impact that environment had on my life until many years later.

My dad was forty-nine years old when I was conceived. My mom was thirty-six years old. When I was five years old, my mom was diagnosed with a brain tumor. She had to have surgery immediately. The tumor was the size of an orange. She was in the hospital for over a month and following this surgery needed long-term care. The doctors had told my dad that they did not expect her to live and if she did live, she would be in bed for a long time. I will never forget the day that my dad had to sign for her to have this surgery, not knowing the outcome of what would happen to his wife. During this stressful time in our family, I witnessed my dad praying a lot and showing how strong his faith in God really was. I recall how he always turned to God first. Dad was very concerned about the outcome of my mom; however, he always maintained a positive and loving attitude. He was always there for my mom. Dad never portrayed a sense of discomfort or agony..........instead, he demonstrated peace, love, and joy.

During most of my childhood, my mom was sick. She spent the majority of these years in bed, at the doctor's office, or in the hospital. Throughout these years, my dad lived a life of faith and peace. No matter the situation, he turned first to God. I could **never** get over his sense of calmness during these difficult times. Mom almost died several times and he continued to walk **daily** with God through it all.

Dad was always there to support her emotionally and faithfully. He encouraged her to believe that God would protect her and keep her safe. He did this so simply, but yet so firmly. Although these were difficult and testing times, my dad always shared his love for his family. He constantly and quietly witnessed his own inner strength through God. My dad was not afraid to depend on God daily for his wisdom and mercy to get through these "challenging and complex times." He always had a smile on his face that radiated to everyone around him. His constant strength was felt by anyone he came in contact with. No matter if we were at the grocery store, pharmacy, or at church, he always displayed God's compassion towards others.

Of all the many trials and tribulations that he faced, his faith and love were always evident. No matter the day of the week, circumstance, or situation at hand, he faced each with a strong heart and desire to do God's will.

As time went by, I grew to be more and more amazed by my dad's spirit. We talked a lot about my mom's health. As a young girl, I could not understand why I did not have a "mom" like all of my friends at school. My mom never came and volunteered in the classroom, baked homemade cookies, or any of the "mom things" that I witnessed around me. This hurt. I shared this pain with my dad. He told me to be thankful that she was even "alive." This was tough in a lot of ways. As I look back on my childhood, I realize and understand that my mom was never the same after her surgery. It was difficult as a child of five years of age to understand what was happening. Today as an adult and mom, I accept and realize that it was amazing that she survived this surgery. I know now, in my heart, that she did the **best job she could during those years**.

My dad was very honest with me that he could not explain what or why this had happened to his wife, and my mom. He went on to say that he was committed to take care of her until he left this earth and would do the best job that he could do. He also shared that he was very sorry that she could not be the "mom" to me that he knew that I needed and desired, but he would be the **best dad** he possibly could to me.

My mom's health was not good at all, in fact, at this time she was in bed twenty-four hours a day. However, my dad began each morning with a smile on his face and in his heart. He was eager to begin a new day despite the actual conditions that were placed on him. His spirit and faith with God radiated through him.

Dad took his job very serious and made sure that we were taken care of and provided for. As one can imagine, my mom required a lot of medicine and doctor's visits to ensure her health. We had what today would be considered an "old time" pharmacy where her prescriptions were filled at as needed. I usually went with him to fill these prescriptions. My dad would take this time to sit with me and have an ice cream or an icy cola, etc. These were times that I will never forget because I realized that he did not have to do this for me OR the fact of how joyous and positive he always made these trips.

I can picture sitting with him and he would give me a "mental math problem" to do. For example, "if one scoop of ice cream costs X, then, how much would seven scoops cost?" He always encouraged me to use my mind and taught me that I should be able to mentally do "math" in my mind. In return, he asked me on Sunday's to teach him "new" vocabulary words. This man always wanted to learn and achieve. He constantly reminded me that anything in life that I set my mind to do, I would achieve. Throughout my childhood, my dad consistently supported me in my educational achievements. **I always knew that he believed in me.**

There have been so many challenging times in my life as an adult and mother that I can only imagine how "difficult" and empty my dad must have felt while attending and caring for my mom. Yet, he began his journey each day with a smile, positive attitude, and determined to live that day to God's blessing. He not only had a desire in his heart to fulfill each day, he lived each day to the abundance of God and what God would have him do.

I would like to share with you a typical morning at our house. My dad was always up early each morning ready to take care of his family. The aroma of coffee or cocoa, bacon or sausage, toast, and eggs would carry through the house. We would begin with prayer and talk about the plans for the day. Of course, my day started with school and my dad was off to his job. After school, I came home and checked on my mom. I usually gave her the medications that she needed, prepared something for her to eat, fed her and did anything else that was necessary. I then worked on laundry, daily housekeeping, and other chores. Next, it was time to begin dinner and homework.

It was so important to me to do anything that I could to "help" my mom get well. I actually thought that I could "fix" her and she would be okay. I so much wanted her to be healthy. However, this never happened. I used to "dream" that one day my mom would be well and she would be able to do all of the "normal things" that a mom should be able to do.

I personally believe that God was preparing me at this time in my life for a **"journey of life"** that I would not always **understand "why."** I am so **thankful** that I had dad to teach me although life is not perfect, by believing in God and doing our personal best each day, we achieve God's purpose for our individual lives.

"Be joyful in hope, patient in affliction, faithful in prayer." (Romans 12:12)

Chapter 2

"He has made everything beautiful in its time." (Ecclesiastes 3:11)

The Garden

Dad always grew a garden. No matter what time of year or season, the garden was full of color and life. We had many conversations over the years in "the garden." One of my greatest memories is that dad grew sunflowers for me among the vegetables. They were beautiful. He also had other flowers around. (We would cut fresh flowers and take inside for my mom in hopes of cheering her up.)

There were many **"lessons of life"** taught to me by my dad in the garden over the years. For some reason, this was the place that I would end up with "all of my questions" for him to give me the **"right" answer**. No matter what my question was at the time, he always told me that God understood whatever was on my heart. He **instilled** in me to always turn to our heavenly father with my concerns. I can recall him over and over saying to me that "**God hears all, sees all, and knows**

all." The sense of peace that went over this man was absolutely amazing.

There were times in this garden that I did not share "with words" to my dad what was on my heart. Even so, he sensed without those "words" what I needed to share. It was absolutely remarkable watching him work on the many plants in the garden and at the same time sharing with me his wisdom.

My heart could be broken inside as I would enter the garden and when I left, I would feel so much better. As we talked about what was on my mind, he would very calmly share with me how he felt.

I enjoyed talking with him because he did not raise his voice, cast judgment, or make me feel worse.

A very special time for dad was after he had farmed with the same gentleman for thirty-two years; he began working for our local extension university. Dad worked with a group of men who were at the doctoral level. They were all amazed at his knowledge of growing a variety of plants, cross-pollination, and simply farming. These men used to actually negotiate over their time with dad. He thoroughly enjoyed this time spent with these men and this extension. I loved hearing his stories at the end of a day about what he had **"taught"** and developed that day. It was nice to hear and see the joy in his heart.

Through the years of spending time with dad while he gardened, he sowed many seeds of life, and at the same time sowed values and morals that **centered around God** and his teachings. I cannot imagine my life today and yesterday without the time spent in the garden. (Dad, thank you…)

"You have made known to me the path of life; You will fill me with joy in your presence." (Psalm 16:11)

Chapter 3

"Be completely humble and gentle; be patient, bearing with one another in love." (Ephesians 4:2)

Environment

Although the setting for our family was the three of us, my dad always made sure that I was with people that would help make a **difference** in my life. One of those special people that he encouraged me to be around was my Aunt Jo. She was actually my great aunt on my mother's side of the family. (I was named after her).

I felt comfortable in our garden one day to ask my dad a question that had been on my heart for some time. I wanted to know why my parents never had other children prior to my birth. He sadly shared that they had tried. They actually lost three children before I was born. Dad even shared there were times that they were not sure mom would be able to deliver me. He said that he did a lot of praying. (I am told that the day that I was born he was a very joyous man).

Aunt Jo never had any children of her own. However, she was always very interested in my life and took a personal interest in me. It was always such a joy to be around her and in her presence. I value all of the lessons and teachings about life that she so **generously taught** me. (I have tried to share and pass on these same virtues to my sons.)

My dad always planted a spring garden for her. We (the three of us) would travel to visit her as often as possible. She was a very warm and strong lady. I always had a tremendous amount of respect for her. This remarkable lady spent time with me teaching me how to cook, shared with me so many life lessons, including constantly encouraging me to get an education outside of high school, to be a lady, and always strive to do my personal best.

After my mom's brain surgery, she spent as much time with me as possible trying to help me understand what was going on. She explained to me that my mom's health would probably never be the same again. Aunt Jo reminded me that life sometimes throws us "curve balls" that we do not have control over. At the same time, she told me to always choose to do what would be right in God's eyes.

I can recall her sharing with me that life was "not perfect for anyone." Honestly, as a young girl, I felt many times that I had been cheated. However, if I truly carried God's spirit in my heart; I could not blame, nor make excuses. It was time to access (even as a young girl) that I was responsible for my choices. I had to accept that I could not blame God or anyone for that matter for my mom's health, growing up without siblings, or any of life's events that occurred.

It was time to move forward and make choices for a brighter future. This meant that school was and continued to be a top priority. I am thankful for teachers that made a difference in my education and my life. Along the way, they took a personal interest in me and encouraged me to strive to become a teacher.

With my dad's support, Aunt Jo, teachers, and people from church, I knew that one day I would be a teacher. It was important to me to make a difference in children's lives.

"Cast your cares on the Lord and He will sustain you; He will never let the righteous fall." (Psalm 55:22)

Chapter 4

"Encourage one another and build each other up, just as in fact you are doing." (1 Thessalonians 5:11)

Encouragement

As time went by, so many things remained the same, while others changed. I grew older and began to become independent as I started making choices that would affect my future. My dad constantly encouraged me to follow my heart as I recognized that I wanted to become a teacher. (In first grade, I told

Mrs. Dunbar (my first grade teacher), one day I would grow up and become a teacher just like her.)

I lost my Aunt Jo as I entered my teen years. This was hard. She had survived breast cancer. However, she was getting older and developed other health issues. Her husband, my Uncle Tom had passed away prior and she was alone. I am sure that she was lonely living by herself.

I had depended on her for so much emotional support as I was getting into my teen years. At this time I was so sad because she had been like a "grandmother, mother, and best friend," all in one package. This was another tough time for me. I had to dig in deep and remind myself of all of "the lessons" that she had so patiently taught me. I knew that she wanted me to succeed in life and strive for achievement. So, it was time to give myself some "life-long pep talks." This is exactly what I did.

As I entered high school, I naturally wanted to do more social activities. However, my time was limited due to my mom's health. (Mom's long-term care continued through these years.) During this time I also began to realize how all of these years must have drained my dad.

Yet, he did not show this. Instead, he continued to witness to me by his daily "walk of faith."

As I reflect back, I clearly see that although my mom was very sick throughout most of my childhood, God placed people in my pathway to make a life-long difference for me, personally. I simply had to choose to tap into these people and allow them to make a difference for me. It was very difficult at times to stay strong. However, in my heart and spirit, it had been planted very deeply at a young age not to ever give up. Without the people in my life that also chose to care and guide me as I grew up, I would not be who I am today. I am most thankful to all of these people that loved and cared about me.

"The heart of the discerning acquires knowledge; the ears of the wise seek it out." (Proverbs 18:15)

Chapter 5

"Let love and faithfulness never leave you...write them on the tablet of your heart." (Proverbs 3:3)

Memories

My childhood memories are different than a lot of children that I grew up with. Most of my friends had siblings, cousins, aunts/uncles, grandparents, and both parents very healthy. I on the other hand did not have a lot of this. There were a lot of times that I truly did not understand why my life was this way. When I went to school, it felt safe, secure, and warm. I felt like I was surrounded by warmth. Due to my mom's health, I did not attend kindergarten, as this was when she had her surgery. I would stand at the window and watch the yellow school bus as it went by. I so much looked forward to attending school and learning all that I could.

When I went to first grade, I was excited to learn how to read, write neatly, and do math. I wanted to make everyone proud of me. However, at the same time on my heart and mind, I worried that when I would arrive home from school would mom still be alive. When I thought of her at school, I prayed and asked God to keep her safe. My first grade teacher used to take a group of us out each morning to feed the birds. This always reminded me of dad in the garden. I would quietly pray to God and ask him to keep my family safe and together. (I worried that if something should suddenly happen to dad, my mom was so sick, what would happen to me? I really wanted to talk to someone about this. I chose to pray.)

While mom was in the hospital having her first surgery, someone gave me a book about a bear. During the time that she was in the hospital, I learned how to read this book. My dad listened to me read this book over and over and over and over. I loved this story. I felt like I had accomplished something very special. I looked so forward to reading this story with my mom once she woke up from feeling bad. Immediately at this time, I was not able to visit in her actual room. I was too young. Therefore, I had to wait. When I did see her for the first time, she was in a wheel chair. She had a "black thing" on her head. I knew immediately that this was not her hair. (Mom had beautiful charcoal hair.) There was no doubt in my mind that this was not her hair. I walked over to her and gave her a hug. Then, I decided to tip-toe up and started pulling at "this thing" on her head. Quickly, I realized that she had no hair. Dad looked at mom and said that together they should explain somewhat of what had actually taken place. They wanted me to understand, but yet protect me at this time. I remember being told that they had to take her hair off temporarily, that her hair would grow back. I knew in my heart that something serious was going on.

The days ahead were not easy; they were very trying times that I will never forget. For at least a month my mom was in the hospital. I stayed with neighbors, friends, and people from church. I watched my dad go away many days to the hospital. Most nights he was home with me, trying to help me understand what was happening. This is the saddest that I had ever seen my dad's eyes. I gave him hugs and told him how much I loved him. Although I was very young, I knew in my heart that something bad had happened to a lady that he loved so much. He tried to reassure me that everything would be okay. Honestly, he did a good job. As I grew older, I knew and began understanding that he actually faced the death of his wife and the mother of his daughter. From the day of this surgery, mom was never the same. Our lives were never the same either. Her health for many years was a constant factor in our family (the three of us). There were so many doctor's appointments, medications, follow-up surgeries, and just normal day to day care that required a lot of patience and time.

Although there were many sad moments during my childhood, I am thankful for the ones that were happy and precious. One of those memories was when my Aunt Jo began teaching me how to make homemade fudge at the age of five. We continued this cooking lesson for a while because she wanted me to be good at this. I can recall standing in a chair and stirring the chocolate with the sugar and butter continuously. She took time to teach me also how to cook southern fried chicken, make homemade biscuits, standing rib- roast, creamed style corn, bake homemade cookies, and many other dishes. This lady entertained garden clubs, church groups, and other social organizations. Everything she did was very classy and elegant. I learned so much from her during the years.

I am most thankful that my dad provided the opportunity for me to be around her especially during holidays and to be able to learn how to do things properly, such as setting the table and cooking. Beyond these lessons, I value that Aunt Jo shared openly with me that an education was so important for me and choosing a "life-long partner" took time and care. She always shared that daily choices affected the future. Her emphasis on being a lady, speaking and writing correctly, and living this life made a tremendous impact on my life.

We were at her house when the "first men landed on the moon." She made sure that I watched and listened to this entire segment on television. Aunt Jo recognized that this would make a difference in our future for our nation.

As I grew older, I always wanted to one day be married in Aunt Jo's home. She had a beautiful winding stairway that she used to make me practice walking down as a lady. We would talk and laugh about one day I would be married in her home and come down this stairway. This was obviously not in God's plan for my life. (As I shared, Aunt Jo died in my early teen years.) However, I walked away with the memory of her teaching me how to walk, sit, and act as a lady. This is something that today I treasure.

Memories with my dad are amazing for me as my children are now young men. I look back on my childhood and am so thankful for all of the lessons, examples, and gifts that he taught me so that I could pass them on to my children. I am also thankful that he shared his love with my mom all of those years. He taught me that when you are with the right partner in life, you love and adore this person no matter what happens. I thank God today that I am finally with that right individual, my husband and life-long soul mate. (It took me a while to get there. I have to accept that this was on God's timing, not mine.) It was definitely worth the wait.

"Trust in the Lord with all your heart and lean not on your own understanding." (Proverbs 3:5).

Chapter 6

"Wisdom that comes from heaven is…pure…peace-loving, considerate…full of mercy…and sincere" (James 3:17)

Educational Dreams

Dear Dad,

After graduating from high school you encouraged me to go to college. You told me that it was time for me to devote time to myself and get an education. You were very excited when I confirmed that I wanted to be a teacher.

Mary Jo Weegar

College was very different than high school. My eyes opened up immediately. I realized that I had a lot of opportunities awaiting me. While in college I worked as a typist for several of the professors of education. This was a very good experience for me as I was exposed to a lot of good information regarding learning and teaching children.

I am very thankful that I had the opportunity to go to college and pursue my dream of becoming a teacher. Thank you for always reminding me that I could do anything that I wanted to do.

With your constant interest in me striving to do my best, this made a difference for me. I remember in high school how you would listen to me when I had essays due. Usually on Sunday afternoon's I would recite my presentation as you sat and patiently listened to me rehearse. This was special for me and let me know that you cared.

One of my greatest memories, dad, was teaching you new vocabulary words on Sunday afternoons. I remember the day that you shared with me that you were not able to get the education in school that you would have liked to accomplish.

I was in elementary school when you told me this story. You shared that you were the youngest of the children in your family and at home when both of your parents took sick. As time went by, you had also been drafted for the war that was going on in our country at the time. You were not at all bitter of taking care of your parents, only thankful that you were able to do this.

At this time I learned that you were only able to complete the fourth grade. You told me that you had to stop school and work in the fields to help provide for your family. I was so amazed. I could not get over this because you could do math in your head faster than anyone I knew. When we went to the grocery store you knew exactly how much money our groceries would cost once we arrived at the checkout. This was awesome.

What you wanted and desired to learn was how to read and write better. It was very important to you to learn new words and their meanings. Over the years on Sunday afternoons especially, we spent time reading and writing. I actually used to give you spelling tests. This was something that I will always treasure. Your desire to learn never stopped.

Thank you for giving me this opportunity to teach you. However, I must admit that over the years what you taught me is something that money cannot buy and is not taught in the average classroom.

Dad, the life long lessons that you shared with me are what have carried me through many years of my life. I recall how you used to go into the fields and put salt tablets under the black peoples' tongues when they had passed out from the heat. You always worked along side with **everyone** and looked out for **anyone**. Your willingness to be a part of any environment never ceased to amaze me. I remember on Friday's how you brought all of the field workers to our house for "pay day." I always had peanut butter and jelly sandwiches, along with ice-cold lemonade for them. They always smiled and enjoyed this treat. I loved doing this for them because it put a smile on their faces and made their tummy feel better.

Another neat memory for me was when you farmed with the local magistrate (thirty-two years actually), and sometimes I would get to go with you to the court house where his office was. You had to go over choices of seeds and other farming information with him. At this time the black people were not allowed to go to the same water fountain or restroom as white people. I would sneak out of the office where you were talking and go get the little white cups by the "white people's water fountain" and fill them up with water. I would carry as many as my little hands could carry and go pass them out to all of the black ladies and gentlemen I could find. Eventually, you would discover that I was not sitting in the chair waiting for you. You would ask the secretary if she knew where I went. She would tell you (with a smile on her face) that I was out "doing my thing." You never got upset with me. This is because you always taught me "to treat others as I would like to be treated." You also emphasized to me over the years that we were all created by God and we were all the same.

Dad, you did not just say these words; you actually lived this example each day of your time on this earth. I can also remember you going and repairing pipes for people in the winter on very cold mornings. They would call on you and you took care of the situation. I remember you cutting wood from trees on our property to give to families so that they had heat for their children. If you had something that would benefit others, you shared.

I can honestly say that in dollar and cents, we were what would be considered poor. However, what you taught me and your time that you spent with me is something that money cannot buy. I have had people tell me many times that my family did an excellent job of raising me because I have manners and I do my best to treat others fairly.

I also appreciate your example of faith in God. You had so many situations when it would have been so easy to be angry and sad. What I witnessed was determination to believe in God no matter what happened. I know in my heart that it must have been very difficult at times during mom's surgery and health situations. However, you never let her see your spirit down. You constantly shared your love for her.

Thank you for being "The World's Greatest Teacher." I have tried and will continue to raise my children by the examples that you raised me by.

My love,

Mary Jo

"Praise be to…God…who comforts us in all our troubles, so that we can comfort those in any trouble." (2 Corinthians 1:3, 4)

Chapter 7

"Create in me a clean heart, O God; and renew a right spirit within me." (Psalm 51:10)

"The fruit of the Spirit is love, joy, peace, patience, kindness, goodness, faithfulness, gentleness…" (Galatians 5:22-23)

Time

Dear Dad,

I must come back and write about the time in my life that I lost you. It was an incredible time for me. In some ways it seems like only yesterday and then I must accept that it was eighteen years ago. This time was hard for me. As a young girl, I used to share with you that when it was time for you to leave this earth that I would not be able to attend your funeral. However, God chose a different plan. I actually planned your funeral. I look back on this and must admit that I am also amazed that I was able to do this. Yet in the end it was such tremendous healing for me.

I recently wrote to you while waiting for Andrew to begin a Symphony performance, about the day that I came to say good-bye to you. I would like to share this experience. It was very special for me.

I was approximately five months pregnant with your second grandchild at this time. We had attended mass this particular Sunday morning. (My doctor had told me that I needed to take a break from visiting every day after school and rest my body during this previous week.) On this Sunday however, I announced that I had to come to visit with you once leaving church.

After arriving at the hospital, I went to leave Andrew, as he was only two, so that I could visit with you. Andrew did not understand why he could not come with his "mommy." I had to explain to him that this was one time that he could not be with me. He did not understand as I walked away from him and approached the double doors leading into intensive care where you were located.

On this day, dad, I knew in my heart that I was coming to say good-bye to you. I prayed all during mass that God would give me the strength not only in my voice, but also in my heart that I could pull this off. You were always so sensitive to my voice and not to mention my "eyes."

I was greeted at the double doors by the nurses that were caring for you. They suggested that I not go in due to the fact that they had wrapped your body as a **mummy**. They also shared with me that they did not want to see me go into premature labor and possibly lose my baby. I told them that I was strong and that I could handle this. You would have been proud of me, as this was a good stubborn moment for me.

Dad, when I entered your room, I could not believe my eyes. I asked the nurses to walk away to the corner of the room and give me some space. They reminded me that I could not touch you. I did not listen…………..I took your hand, and began talking to you.

At this time, I thanked you for being my "dad." I reminded you of the "talks" over the years in the garden, you taking me to pick cotton when I was five years old, listening to me, saying the "Lord's Prayer," each night with me, telling me that I could not play football with the boys anymore (when I did not understand why), most importantly being "YOU."

I also told you that your new grandchild would not be a girl. It was so important to me to name a little girl after you, "Jessica Whitney." This was obviously not in God's plan, which is okay. At this time, I shared with you that this child was a boy and that I had chosen to name him after your dad, Benjamin Joseph. I squeezed your hand because this meant so much to me, and in my heart I had to accept that you would not hold and feed this grandchild. I was sad. While feeling this sadness, you squeezed my hand back..........I knew that you heard every word that I was saying. Before I left your room, you fluttered your eyes at me. I felt blessed to be able to share these important thoughts with you.

There was so much more that I wanted to share with you on this day. Yet, I knew that I had to be strong and I had to hold on. For once in my life I could not honestly share with you dad what I yearned deep in my heart to talk with you about. I had to hold on and believe that God would hear me. This was such a tough time for me. Dad, I was losing you. I could not fix or repair you. I did not understand how and why God was taking you from me when I felt that I needed you more than ever. (As I write these words, I can today picture looking at you............I only wanted to take you home with me and make you better............I could not............... God wanted you with him..............) I kissed you on the forehead and told you to go and be with the Lord, where you so naturally deserved to be.

I treasure and value this last conversation with you. Although it was not easy, I cherish these last moments with you. On this last day on earth, you gave me the last lesson and gift that I would need to get me through the next few years, the toughest time of my life. This lesson was confirmed by you and your spirit that I should always depend on God for everything. Dad, I had to do exactly that for a while. It was not easy, but I did it, because of YOU.

I love you dad,

Mary Jo

Mary Jo Weegar

"But if we love one another, God lives in us and his love is made complete in us."
(1 John 4:12)

Saying Good-bye..................

Dear Dad,

Saying good-bye to you is something that I feel in my heart I have never actually done. As I have written earlier in this book, I had to be extremely strong during your death due to being pregnant with your second grandchild. It was the Christmas season also.

At this time, I was teaching second grade. I had twenty-nine second grade students. They were all very kind during the twenty-two days that you were in the hospital. We would go to mass each week from school and they would share with me on the way back that they had said a special prayer for you. This always warmed my heart.

I was teaching the day that you died. (This was the day after I had visited you.) Approximately 9:20 in the morning I was teaching reading. I had looked up at the clock and had a feeling in my heart that you had just died………..you did. My principal had received the call that morning; however, she did not tell me until the end of the school day. I remember feeling so empty. It was like I could not feel what was happening. From school I left and went to the funeral home to take care of your arrangements. It was amazing to me as I was planning and making decisions regarding your funeral as how strong my spirit and heart felt. I even said out loud that I could not believe how I was able to do this. I knew that this was God giving me exactly what I needed to get through this time.

Your funeral was beautiful. The church was packed and there were people even outside of the church. The service began with music and everyone saying together "The Our Father Prayer." This was very important to me because you always knelt down and said this prayer with me when I was a young girl and throughout the years. Today, this prayer is still very important to me and a part of my life with my family.

When I returned to school after your death, my students were very warm and glad to see me. They had hand made twenty-nine flowers with a beautiful ribbon and had arranged them on the wall near the reading area. I could not get over this. They were so kind and thoughtful. These children let me know quickly that they were ready to learn and get back to business. Their loving spirits began helping me to move forward after this sad time. I was most grateful.

The year progressed and I stayed very busy with school and being a mom. On May 4, 1989, your second grandson was born. His name is Benjamin Joseph. He was very healthy and strong. Ben is now a senior in high school. He is a very talented young man. God has blessed

Ben with his hands. He does hard wood flooring, tile work, plumbing, electrical, carpentry, and most anything he makes his mind up to do. He has learned how to do all of these things by watching home improvement programs and reading books on these trades.

Andrew is almost twenty years old. He is in his second year in college. Andrew is very talented also. His major is psychology and he wants to work with children with learning disabilities. Andrew is very sensitive to people and children. He always tries to help anyone that comes his way.

God has blessed me with both of these young men. I am so sorry that you were not able to be here on this earth and watch them grow up. However, I have shared with them everything that I possibly could about you, especially the "lessons of life" that you taught me when I was a young girl.

My last visit with you on your front porch was the day before you went into the hospital. Andrew and I came down to visit with you. (Ben was not born yet..... I was five months pregnant with him.)

Dad, I knew that you were not feeling well this day because you did not come out to the car and get Andrew out of his car seat like you normally did. However, you met me on the porch and held Andrew in your arms while we visited. You looked very weak on this day, yet you asked me several times if everything was okay. I said yes, although things were not okay. You even asked me to look into your eyes and tell you that I was okay. I could not do this. On this day you sensed something was not right. However, I could not tell you how heavy my heart and spirit actually was.

There were many times that I "chose to protect you" from events that were not good because I loved you so much. I did not want to add to your "worry" because your plate was already full with mom's health issues. As a child, she did many things to me that I kept in my heart. I shared with you as little as I possibly had to because I did not want your health to go down. For example, she cut most of my hair off one day while I was cutting out paper dolls. It was storming outside and Aunt Jo had given me some paper dolls that I was cutting and decorating. Mom said that I was making too much noise with the scissors. She grabbed these huge scissors and began forcefully cutting my hair. (My hair was down almost to my bottom before she did this.) You were not pleased when you got home and saw what she had done. You talked with her for a long time in a calm, but firm manner. I never told you this, but she also told me that I would never become a teacher. She told me that I would not make it through college. I chose to hold onto what you taught me………..I could do anything that I set my mind to. You will be pleased to know that I am currently in my twenty-fifth year of teaching.

There were also other moments of my life that I chose not to share with you. I did not want you to worry about me. When I was in college, I was almost raped. I was able to get away after being scratched, bruised, and battered by this person. I feel blessed that God put people in my pathway to help me escape from this individual. I did not tell you because I loved you so much.

After graduating from college I remember sharing with you that my first job would be teaching fourth grade. You were so excited for me. We both knew why fourth grade was a special grade level, didn't we?

After teaching for a couple of years, I married. I lived unfortunately in a very controlled environment. It was difficult for me to be able to come and visit with you as I would have liked to over the years. You know that as time went by, I visited less. I wish that I could take that time back..........

My first marriage was not at all what I thought it would have been. However, God blessed me with two beautiful sons from this marriage. As the years went by, the boys and I became very close and learned how to "survive together the storms" that we faced. There were many difficult moments. Dad, this is a time that I would have loved to come and talked with you to help me understand. I had to depend on God and remember to dig in deep to some of those life lessons that you taught me as a young girl. These were some very tough years for me. I tried to put all of my energy into my children and teaching. I did a lot of praying. I lived in so much fear each day at this time. Actually, I was consumed with fear. I prayed over and over that God would keep me safe so that I could raise my children. Today I look back and deep down in my heart I know that the way I survived those years had a lot to do with "your teachings, value system, and love." In my heart I knew that what I was experiencing was very wrong. However, I could not get out of this situation until I knew it was safe. You always taught me to talk to God, believe me I did just that. At the same time, I knew that you had raised me not to ever allow fear to take over me. However, it did. I am sorry. I could not turn to just anyone with what was happening.

God blessed me with a very special lady that I taught school with. We actually met and got to know each other after she was having a diabetic attack. I was working in my classroom and heard someone across the hallway gasping. It was her. I ran over and did not know exactly what was happening. I took a guess and prayed that I was doing what was necessary. I ran down stairs in the basement and purchased a soda. When I went back upstairs, I lifted her head and began pouring soda down her throat. She started sitting up and was coming back around. We instantly bonded. This special lady has been a large part of my life ever since. I refer to her as "my mom away from home." Her name is "Miss Graham." She used to travel with me when you were in the hospital. I went through a tremendous storm and I am thankful this lady was there for us. She even saved mine and Ben's lives when I was pregnant with him. "Miss Graham" has been a tremendous support for me over time. Eventually, I went to her and shared what was going on. I knew that I could trust her and rely on her wisdom. She was very concerned and worried about my safety and well-being. "Miss Graham" also told me to pray and constantly ask God's blessings. She traveled through "many storms" with me. I cannot imagine my life without her love. Like you, she always believed in God's blessings for his children. She used to tell me that God had a plan and special purpose for my life and not to give up.

There were many times that it would have been very easy to do just that. In fact, next to your death, this was probably the most dramatic time in my life. I had to stay strong for the boys and be able to go to my job. There were many times that I honestly thought that death would be easier than having to endure and get through this "mess." You always seemed to be able to survive any of the many circumstances that were placed upon you with mom. I could never understand how you did it. (You were so loving, kind, and generous with your spirit for her; yet, it felt like it was taken for granted.) Dad, I have survived so much. I could not have done so without those years of your teachings. I am so thankful that I "recorded and held on to these lessons of life."

As time went by, life was quite a challenge. It felt good at the end of each day to have survived and then to wake up the next morning. When my children were safe and sound, I felt blessed. We became what I would describe as a "triangle unit." This is a positive that developed from something not so good. The three of us relied on each other for strength, prayer, and peace.

After a storm usually the skies are a beautiful blue. Well dad, I am fortunate and blessed to say that I made it through some major storms. I am also blessed that God indeed held me in the palm of his hand and had a better plan and purpose for my life. This blessing was not only for me, but also Andrew and Ben. His name is Timothy Edward Weegar.

Dad, within a few days of meeting Tim, he sent me a beautiful bouquet of "mixed live flowers." I could not believe my eyes! This was a surprise for me. Below, is the note that was attached to the flowers. (Immediately, I felt blessed by God.)

MaryJo
You're the Worlds' greatest "TeacheR"
And an awesome blessing from GoD.
Thinking of you,
Tim

I met Tim on October 21, 2001 in a local Baptist church study group. On November 21, 2001, Tim asked me to marry him. We were married on December 21, 2001 in my home. Tim was friends with a federal judge and he, along with our associate pastor married us. A lot of our friends, neighbors, and his family shared this beautiful ceremony with us. Dad, this day was perfect! We have just recently celebrated our fifth wedding anniversary. These five years have been amazing.

You would absolutely adore Tim. He is a man of God and very gentle. A lot of his character is like you. I wish that you could have met Tim before leaving this earth. However, I feel that you know about him. Even so, I wish that you could come shake his hand, have dinner, and fellowship with us. I constantly try to share your "love of life," spirit and your constant gentleness.

Dad, you were such an awesome man, yet you were always so quiet. You never brought praise among yourself and/or accepted anyone trying to bring you into the "spotlight." I miss you terribly; however, I thank God daily for having a DAD such as you were. Although you are not still here on this earth, I know you are "here" with me.

I actually started a book prior to this one. However, before I can "go" there, I have to give you praise for your awesome

"Gift of Teachings." I love you DAD! God bless you.

I love you so much, I miss you terribly; however, I am so proud of you for being with our "Heavenly Father" where you so naturally deserve to be. Again, thank you for being my DAD and daily showing your love for life.

It has been very important to me to share with you that I am safe and very happy. I could not ask for God to have picked a more loving husband and healthy father for my children.

It is nice to share with you that I am safe and happy. God bless you, dad.

My love,

Mary Jo

"These three remain: faith, hope, and love. But the greatest of these is love." (1 Corinthians 13:13)

About the Author

Mary Jo Weegar is married to Timothy E. Weegar. She is the proud mom of two sons, Andrew and Ben. Mary Jo graduated from the University of South Carolina in 1981, with a degree in Early Childhood Education. She was Teacher of the Year for the 1999-2000 academic year. Mary Jo has written many educational grants over the years for classroom materials. Currently, she is in her twenty-fifth year of teaching. Mary Jo, along with her husband, Tim, both serve on her local School Improvement Council.

Mary Jo enjoys cooking, reading, writing, learning to play the piano, and spending time with her family.

She especially enjoys making candlelight dinners with peaceful music playing for her family. Mary Jo looks forward to the bonding that always naturally occurs during dinner with her family.

Printed in the United States
76251LV00001B/100-120